Loving Him

By

Patara Thompson

Copyright © 2007 by Patara Thompson

Loving Him
by Patara Thompson

Printed in the United States of America

ISBN 978-1-60034-950-8

All rights reserved solely by the author. The author guarantees all contents are original and do not infringe upon the legal rights of any other person or work. No part of this book may be reproduced in any form without the permission of the author. The views expressed in this book are not necessarily those of the publisher.

Unless otherwise indicated, Bible quotations are taken from New Living Translation version of the Bible. Copyright © 2004 by Tyndale House Publishers, Inc.

www.xulonpress.com

Dedication

This book is dedicated to all those who have ever felt unloved and unwanted. It may seem as though you have been abandoned in life. I submit to you that there is a Man who found me in the same state as you presently are or may have been at some point. Because of what He did, I am still loving Him. According to Ezekiel 16:4-14, the Lord declares, "On the day you were born, no one cared about you. Your umbilical cord was not cut, and you were never washed, rubbed with salt, and wrapped in cloth. No one had the slightest interest in you. No one pitied you or cared for you. On the day you were born, you were unwanted, dumped in a field and left to die. But I came by and saw you there, helplessly kicking about in your own blood. As you lay there, I said, "Live!" And I helped you to thrive like a plant in the field. You grew up and became a beautiful jewel. Your breasts became full, and your body hair grew, but you were still naked. And when I passed by again, I saw that you were old enough for love. So I wrapped my cloak around you to cover your

Loving Him

nakedness and declared my marriage vows. I made a covenant with you, says the Sovereign Lord, and you became mine. Then I bathed you and washed off your blood, and I rubbed fragrant oils into your skin. I gave you expensive clothing of fine linen and silk, beautifully embroidered, and sandals made of fine goatskin leather. I gave you lovely jewelry, bracelets, beautiful necklaces, a ring for your nose, earrings for your ears, and a lovely crown for your head. And so you were adorned with gold and silver. Your cloths were made of fine linen and were beautifully embroidered. You ate the finest foods-choice flour, honey, and olive oil-and became more beautiful than ever. You looked like a queen, and so you were! Your fame soon spread throughout the world because of your beauty. I dressed you in my splendor and perfected your beauty, says the Sovereign Lord."

Acknowledgements

To Staci Williams

I am grateful to God for sharing interesting times with you, such as laying hands on a television that was not working and believing by faith that it would. To our amazement, it actually worked! Faith with out works is indeed dead. Thank you for your two-second recipe ideas and home remedies, of which I seem to always be the recipient. I love you a bushel and a peck and a hug around the neck.

To Laila Thompson and Nicole Darko

Thank you for being my family. You have been true sisters in my life. You were there for me during dark times. I love you girls so much. Where ever I go in the world, from France to Africa, please know you will always have a place in my home. While our husbands go to the football game and our children play, we will sip tea and talk about old times. Wow! I can't wait.

Loving Him

To Tonya Chandler

Thank you for your beautiful voice when you speak. Often times, I tell you that your voice has a musical quality because it is very soothing. I appreciate the unusual friendship we have. There is no one else with whom I have this type of friendship. To someone on the outside, it may seem as though we say some pretty horrible things to each other. We seem to have this unspoken understanding of each other. Now, don't get the wrong idea that I like you because of what I am saying here. That is not the case at all. I love you, girl.

To Tracy Cooper

Thank you for being the following to me: driver, counselor, financial advisor, Sunday school teacher, cook, dishwasher, doctor and nurse. Also, thank you for your love, support, honesty, sincerity, integrity, concerns, prayers, shelter, knowledge of music, clothes and shoes. You really don't know a person unless you live with them. You probably know me more than any one else in the earth because we have lived together. Child, we have grown. I enjoy our times of sharing. My favorite times are Sundays after church. We have really deep conversations about so many things. We laugh and cry. The awesome thing is sometimes I plant and you water or you plant and I water. We just flow as the Holy Spirit leads. We both grow. Please know I will always have your back. We are in covenant. I love you very much.

Loving Him

To my Aunt Mary Rushing, who was the epitome of what holiness is and my momma. Thank you for your soft, squishy hugs.

To my Aunt Kathy Stokes

Thank you for your love of cars, especially the fast ones. I, too, love them. I remember very vividly our trips down deep into the "country" when I was a little girl. We would load up your car and take off. We always made a stop at Mr. Jess' country store to buy Vienna sausages, sardines, and crackers. Oh, I dare not forget about bologna with "light" bread and hook cheese. To wash that cheese down, we would drink ice cold cokes in the old "el bottles". When you placed your arm out the window, I knew we were getting ready to fly. As my mother sat up front, she complained that you needed to slow down. I wanted you to gun it even faster. You had no clue that there was little girl sitting in the back seat filled with glee because of the way her Aunt Cadillac hugged those curves. Now that I am a young woman, I appreciate those times even more than when I was a child. Thank you.

To Elsie Covington

Thank you also for being my mother and looking forward to my phone calls.

To my mentor in the gospel, Vivian Humphrey, who is an awesome Godly woman. You are indeed God's woman. A lot of people claim to know God, but does

He claim to know them? When you are flying, look down 'cause I've got your dress tail.

To Pastors William T. and Glendora Ford
    Thank you for a heart for worship.

To Pastors Patrick and Mary Pinckney
    Thank you for your youthful zest and vision for life.

To Joseph's House,
    Thank you for igniting the fire in me.

Forward

LOVING HIM is truly an expression of worship to God the Father, the maker of heaven and earth, who is all knowing and sovereign in all things. When reading this worship experience, there is such liberty and understanding of who Jesus Christ is. There is such freedom and deliverance that Jesus, the epitome of love, has given all of us.

As you read LOVING HIM, you will be reminded of the call to worship in "spirit and truth." John 4:23 declares that: "But the time is coming-indeed it's here now-when true worshipers will worship the Father in spirit and truth. The Father is looking for those who will worship him that way". This passage of scripture reveals that God is ALIVE and desires our fellowship to be with Him, just by the mere fact that He is seeking (presently). Jesus Christ came that we may have life and that our lives be restored back to the Father. When we worship in spirit and truth, we understand God's unchanging love for us. This love cannot be understood until experienced.

Reading LOVING HIM will cause your heart to be open, and your mind to receive from Christ Jesus Himself. It also gives you an understanding of the awesome power of the Holy Spirit. When we can fathom God's love, we understand that we are more than a conquer and we understand that God will never forsake us. We understand the anointing and power that we have only through Christ Jesus. Jesus Christ loves us so much and is waiting with opened arms to restore us back to the Father.

My prayer is you would open your heart and receive Jesus today; allow HIM to change you and your situations through a worship experience.

With Love,
Staci Williams

A Personal Word from the Holy Spirit

To Patara With Love

I love thee all the day long as the day is far gone. I shall love you until the evening comes. Put your trust in Me, my child, and do not frown. The devil is a clown. He wants you to be sad and down. I love you, Patara Brooks. I Am the One who created you back in '76. Yea, I made you. Allow Me to come inside and reside in you. I will speak words of wisdom to you. Just for you will I do it. Oh precious child, understand that no one can separate the love that I have for you. My heart for you is true. Allow not the devil to whisper in thine ears or to work up or awake all thy fears. You need to control it by casting such thoughts in the fire. Hey girl, you are My heart's desire. Imagine, just for a moment, our walking through the meadows.. through the green grass as it glistens from the heat of the day. We listen to the larks sing sweet songs of heaven. We walk hand in

Loving Him

hand because this is a bond that is unbreakable. This is a bond that no other man can understand or withstand. Imagine. I look into your eyes as I impart into you. We make love until evening comes and until the owl says, "Who". I love you, Patara Brooks, more than any man could love you. You are in Me and I am in you. Together we shall grow old. Silence the voice of the enemy that whispers that I don't love you. Even when the day is far spent and the clouds of a new day approach, My love for thee can never ever be broken.

I speak to you, Patara, when you least expect. Never allow the enemy to say it is I who neglect. I speak to you early in the morning and late in the evening. In this time are the secrets from My heart to yours established in heaven and earth. No one can change what I have spoken in your heart. I speak to you every minute when you think that I'm not. I am speaking to you to help you to go through. Don't you remember? You are my prize possession. Allow Me to make that to be established in you, for it is already in heaven. Allow Me, Patara, to wear all of your burdens around my neck. My Son dying on the cross has that already set. Believe in Me as you sit here to type. Allow My words to fill your heart. It is I that speak to you. Even now the words that you hear are My sound. You are filled with words…words that testify of Me. Do not be burdened by this gift. Why do you cry as you sit here to type what I speak to your heart? The Word declares that true worshipers will worship Me in Spirit and in Truth. Listen for Truth. Truth is unwavering, unmovable and pure in

Loving Him

thought. That is Me. I'll teach you. You need only to rest in Me like you would on a pillow and take heart. Remember? This is what Truth sounds and feels like. I am the Living Waters constantly flowing in you. Drink of Me, Patara. Don't let the water be stagnant. Patara, drink of Me and be engrossed by Me. Patara, take notice of the infilling that I bring. You have Me in the palms of your hands. I am Water that won't run through your fingers. I have form, life and abundance…..The Living Waters. Patara, drink of Me and learn of Me by casting all of your burdens aside. I Am the Good Shepherd and Gracious Host. Allow Me to lead you in the drinking of Me…..The Living Waters. Don't be hesitant in worshiping Me in Spirit and Truth. I have taught you well. You know what to do. As a tree knows what to do in the mist of wind, so do you know what to do when My Presence is upon you . Learn of Me and eat of Me. Eat this bread that will cause no hunger to come upon you, but will give life everlasting for which you do yearn.

    Lovingly,
    Holy Spirit

Introduction

This book is the summation of my love for Him….. Jesus. You know, today a lot of people use His name so loosely. His name virtually has become a part of the every day language of the saint and sinner alike. There are so many people who do not have an intimate relationship with Him.

Unfortunately, that includes some believers. As you read my book, I would like for you to focus on Him and not on issues that so easily beset you: Sunday religion, titles, positions, slothful saints, lawlessness in the world, bills, dead end jobs, what you want, your previous abuses, loneliness, the fact that you were adopted, raped, and hated with out cause, just to name a few. Those of you that are angry with God, please open your heart. I invite you to go with me on a trip as I paint with words the vivid images of my Lover. I want you to be with me while I am loving Him with out restraint. Please come with me as I love the lover of my soul. This book is not for believers or non-believers. It is for those who have a dry, parched thirst for Him, and are willing to give it all to have a

Loving Him

drink of His nectar. This book is not for a particular race. The love that this Man gives transcends all of the boundaries or limitations that human beings have concocted to keep us separated. Allow the Spirit of God to teach you how to know him through your spiritual senses. He is there. He wants to embrace you as you bask in His presence. He is waiting to hear you. Once you really see this Man behind the name that we tend to use so loosely, you will see love- I mean a love that is pure, tranquil, peaceful, and free….far beyond free. If no one has ever told you that they love you, you should begin to give love. I admonish you to begin loving Him right now. How do you do that, you may ask? You need to call His name until you can feel freedom in your heart. You will sense overwhelming love flowing into your heart. His love is pure. He will never lie to you, nor will He ever hurt you. He is the exact expression of love. You don't have to be at church or any particular place before you meet Him intimately. He is waiting to hear from you.

Contents

Dedication v
Acknowledgements vii
Foreword.. xi
A Word from the Holy Spirit xiii
Introduction... xvii

Section I: Psalms
A Refreshing 22
Let Go and Let God 23
A part of Him 24
The Comforter..25
It's Morning 26
Reality Dream 27
Pray 28
In Time 30
Never Alone 31
My Lord's...32
Heaven 33
One Day 34
O' Lord...35
The Quencher...36
True Beauty..37
Narrow and Rocky Road 38

Life 39
True Friend 40

Section II: Warrior
Brave Warrior 42
More Than A Conqueror 44
Release 45
He Reigns 46
Sick and Tired 47
Battle Cry 48
The Evangelist 49
The Promise 52
The Experience 54

Section III: Worship
Prophetic Worship 56
The Kiss 58
The New Jerusalem 59
The Marriage 60
Heavenly Melodies 61
The Worship of God 62
Dance 64
Golden Rays 65
I'm Here 66
Divine Perseverance 67
Momma Died 68
Unhindered Love 69
Worship 71
Healing Virtue 72
The Triumph of Jesus 73

Psalms

A Refreshing

Breathe upon us, oh Holy Spirit and reveal to us who we are to be.
Plant a seed in us dear God so that we can
receive power.
Flow within us, oh Holy Spirit with a flow that will cause us to grow.
Anoint us from on high with your presence that will cause us to supernaturally glow.
Refresh us with heavenly rain for Jesus came to set us free.
Give us the desire to proclaim this liberty.
Oh God, as I lift my hands to worship, you wash away the pain.
Thank you for your refreshing rain.

Let Go and Let God

Let go and let God lead and guide you.
He will lead and guide you the right way.
All He asks us to do in repay is to let Him be the only God, and do unto others as we would have them do unto us.
Let go and let God use your soul and mind to help this world be a better place to live in. Let go and let God hold your hand for He will never let you fall.

A Part of Him

I am a part of Jesus Christ, and He is a part of me. Together forever we shall be. Never will I have to stand alone, for when He died on the cross, His true love He has shown.

Loving Him

The Comforter

Like rushing rivers the Holy Spirit consumes me. He destroys the yoke of the enemy so that I can be free.
He opens me up and helps me to see the world through his eyes and who I am destined to be.
He fills and over takes me by his presence.
He overflows me so much, I feel like I'm in Heaven.
The Holy Spirit rebukes me when I am wrong, but always comforts me with a song.
He wraps me with his tender loving arms of grace.
He speaks mysteries to me….sweet promises that words can never say.
So comfortable in this comfortless world, He is able to make me feel. Living with the Holy Spirit is indeed a thrill.
It is only through Him that I can truly be real.

It's Morning

A new day is dawning. In the mist of it,
I am yawning.
I am awakening from a sleep of desolation and desperation. The overflowing powers of God capture the essence of this awakening.
A new day has dawned. I was weak and now
I am strong.
My tongue has He loosed like Zacharius to proclaim the glory of the Lord.
A new day is dawning and has dawned.
Come see, all ye, the birth of the new fawn… see her scamper and glimmer in the brightness of the Son.
A whole new world is she compelled to go and view because she has accepted what God has called her to do.

Reality Dream

Crystally beautiful is He who lives in me.
My Heavenly Father is no mystery. He came to me one night all in a clear glowing white.
His arms were outstretched wide to let me know He is on my burden-bearing side.
His face was full of sunny glory.
Words can not express my true Heavenly story.

Pray

God, teach us how to pray.
Open our hearts and minds to know what to say.
Direct us dear Lord so that our prayer may go through, and we will know what to do. Hover over us, Holy Spirit, like a bee over a flower and quench us with your never-ending fire.
God, deliver us from all that is within for a prayer can't go up if we are living in sin. Search us, oh Mighty One until Your heart is content.
Fill us the more with the Holy Ghost. Oh yes!
The Comforter you sent.
Fill us with the Holy Ghost from our head to our feet, and saturate us so much we can't keep our seat.
Anoint us, dear God as You anoint the flowers with dew. No evidence is needed for we know that
it is You.
Anoint us like rivers overflowing their banks. We will be sure to give you a hallelujah, praise God, and thanks.
Hosanna, direct us, for we have no one else to turn to.
Lead us, dear God by guiding us with Your rod.
Breathe on us as only you can breathe, for the enemy is trying to sift us out and deceive. Retrieve us from the hands of our enemies for they are many.
Receive us unto You, for in You there is no death.
Rescue us from the snares of that serpent of old. Teach us, God, how to stand bold. Keep us close to your breast so that we can past the test. If we would

only believe and have faith, we know You will do the rest.

In Time

No one knows the hour or the day in which He will come.
He will summon Gabriel to blow his horn loud and clear to let the saints know behold the time is here.
On a gigantic cloud of fluffy white He will indeed come into sight with arms outstretched from sea to sea looking for a church amongst the unbelief.
The saints will then rise into the middle of the air without a care - the ones who dared to believe that He, the Lord Our God, has always been there.
He will then destroy earth with fire and brimstone as sinners cry out for mercy as they reap for what they have sown. Mercy will not be shown, for they did not allow Jesus to become their own.
Pain or sorrow will not be the songs of the saints, but that of redemption and thanks.

Loving Him

Never Alone

The Lord is with me through every step of my life.
He is the shadow that follows me from morning '
til night.
He is the gentle wind that cools me when the humid
day is done.
He is the One that tells me I must fear none.
He is the One that comforts me in times of despair
when I feel no one will care.
He is the One who talks about setting my soul free.
Dear Lord, there is nothing in all Your Father's great
creation like Thee.

My Lord's

My Lord's whispering voice is pleasing to my heart.
I feel full, warm, and so complete inside.
My Lord's presence gives me a sense of living like I can live forever.
My Lord's gentle touch wakes me in the morning and puts me to sleep at night.
My Lord's constant and unchangeable love fills me up so that I overflow with happiness.

Heaven

Heaven is where the streets are laden with gold, and where man never grows old.

Heaven is where singing and shouting goes on every day, and weary and tired spirits play. Heaven is where rejoicing is to the divine, and where such fellowship is to last for all time. Heaven is where the winner of the race finally takes his rest, and where a golden, golden crown is given to the very best. Heaven is where Christ Jesus reigns, and where through thousands and thousands of years He has shouldered our pains.

Heaven is where tranquility lies, and where no one ever dies. Heaven is where I'm going to be, and where all are full of the blessed Holy Spirit like me.

One Day

The Lord is my love.
He has been in the midst of all my dreams and thereof.
With the burdens that the tests of life may throw my way, He is always there to comfort me with the words, "It's okay".
I can't wait 'til I see how heaven is going to be. It will be a home that will never again be a mystery.

O' Lord

Give me Your wisdom O' Lord.
Give it to me one hundred percent.
Give me a kind heart O' Mighty One so that I can show the world there is still good in this sinful place.
Give me Your undying love my Heavenly Father and let it come into my heart peacefully to show people how great Your love truly is.
My sweet, sweet Jesus, continue to mold me and make me.
Most of all, show me the way.

The Quencher

The Lord my God will replenish my soul when in drought. Renewed faith replaces all doubt when Christ comforts me in saying things will work out.

True Beauty

Every beautiful day that I see can never ever surpass the beauty of the Lord my God to me. Crystally beautiful is He.

Narrow and Rocky Road

When walking on a narrow and rocky road, always count on God to take control.
He will hold your hand when no one else can.
He will put faith into your soul when others would just leave you and let go.
God will put joy into your heart and never will He part you.

Life

Life is not what it seems.
Sometimes it is evil and unfair.
While at other times, it is dear and very
truthful to us.
Pray to the one that gives life and not to the one who despises it so.
If you take time to pray to the one that gives life, your own shall be very truthful and most of all everlasting.

True Friend

Beaten, beaten was He who died on the cross for us;
nails of rust driven in this hand and that one.
This was done to the Son.
As blood ran down His face our grace was put
into place.
Stretched out arms and a drooped down head was the
scene as He bled.
His face was purplish blue and red. The crowd of
sinners proclaimed in victory that He was dead.
This was to fulfill what scripture already said.
He got up off His death bed and went down to hell.
He released the captives on Satan's turf.
As Christ freed them, they rejoiced in their rebirth.
He conquered death, hell and the grave so the world
could be saved.

Warrior

Brave Warrior

Lord, help me to hold out.
Trials and tribulations are coming my way so fast it makes me want to shout.
So many troubles on every side, it seems I
cannot bear.
Through Your loving care, I know You'll always
be there.
Sometimes, I just want to block out the world and close my eyes. I want to live my whole life
in a disguise.
Lord, I don't know how to pray, on bended knees, I don't know what to say.
Like David, my sins are constantly before my face.
Lord, please help me to run this Christian race.
You are soon to come, so please haste.
Help me to be ready to be caught up in the middle of the air…. our destination a place with out despair.
Then I heard my Father in Heaven say:
Arise! Arise! For I have laid up for you a
great surprise.
If you work in my vineyard and bear all the things you must bear, the surprise will I give you - my home in glory will I indeed share.
It is a place with out a sun or night for I will be the everlasting, everlasting Light.
I will wipe a way all of your tears and fears.
Your battle scars will I sooth.
No more heartache and pain for this reason was the Lamb slain.

Loving Him

So take heart My child and do not cry for beside you will I be by and by.

More Than A Conqueror

Go back to when you first believed, for in going back, you will receive that fire all over again that pardoned your sin.
There is nothing that the fire can't burn up. Going back to when you first believed will cause
you to shout.
In this shouting, your testimony will be given.
All of Satan's deceiving lies will be brought
to the light.
The fire will cause you to shout yeah, yeah God its going to be alright.

Release

Filling up the pews with wonderment,
Hoping the Holy Spirit will just ease on in when you know you're just sitting there contemplating
about sin.
How could this be for the Lamb died for you
and me?
He made a decree in the land to let my people go.
So understand there are no longer bounds holding you back. Glory!
He has already taken up the slack.
Release yourself oh captive one. Run, run, run so that the Lord's will be done.

He Reigns

Jesus Christ reigns in heaven and earth. He will come with a shout from above as the angels praise and encircle Him with their love. The angels will praise and worship Him with all that is within because of His glorious and majestic being.

People will cry, moan and weep as He opens His mouth to speak. Some will be thrown into the lake of fire while others will come boldly to the throne of grace on the side of the sheep and take their rightful place.

The saints will sing a song that no one else will be able to learn for these are the ones that have laid down their life as far as Jesus is concerned.

Sick and Tired

No longer will hopelessness fill my once desolate soul, for the Word of God has made me bold.
I can't stand to be without His grace, for without it, again sin I'll embrace.
I'm getting frustrated with how the world lives - their having knowledge of Christ dying on the cross, yet going on with fleshy thrills.
They live from one moment to the next, and not realizing totally how God is getting more
and more vexed!
God is continuously holding His peace while Jesus, the advocate, pleads "Wait, Father, please wait... they'll cease."

Battle Cry

He placed my feet on a higher ground.
No longer I'm I bound. Do you see the stitches, marks and strays that the devil has made?
I came to tell ya Jesus has already paid and in that I'm I saved.
For so long have I prayed to be delivered one day.
My flesh does not understand the Holy Spirit's command to jump, shout and praise the Lord as hard as I can.
 I purge myself of praises and glory to Jesus, for He is the Chief Cornerstone.
The Man.
A Man full of power, awesome and might.
He makes you want to get up and take flight, for in this you know, it will be alright. Therefore, don't lose sight of your right to the tree of life. For only through struggle and strife can you win the fight!!!

The Evangelist

Across the seas into a foreign land the gospel of Jesus Christ will I proclaim.
My being defamed is alright as long as the world knows He reigns.

Through Him have I experienced mysteries beyond measure. No words can express the joy and pleasure my God brings me.

Because of the blood of the Lamb, am I now redeemed. I count all things lost for Christ for He was the ultimate sacrifice.
Because of this, I love and adore my risen Christ.

While I was in the world, I was the apple of His Eye. Because of the favor upon my life, even then I couldn't get by.

I often wondered why I couldn't be an ordinary sistah sitting on the pew, clapping my hands, praising God and doing the Holy Ghost dance.

God had a plan for my life.

While in the world, like I said, I was the apple of my Father's eye. He knew then, according to the purpose already established in heaven I would be willing to die.

continued

Loving Him

Abiding in God and His abiding in me is my heart's desire. Becoming like the image of Jesus Christ do I aspire.

No longer am I the old man but the new man that the father foreknew. A focused purpose in me does He now pursue.

I want to be engulfed by the presence of my God. I want to kiss the tears of my Daddy when the world turns its back on His Son.
I want to remind Him of His Word that the work of Jesus Christ has already been established and done.

I want to lye prostrate on the floor, yielding and submitting all of me to Him……
An action that has no depth.

I want to take a spiritual dive in the pool of His glory. I want everything that makes me to be sanctified by His extraordinary Spirit.
I want to go so deep into my Baby that I can hear His heart beat. I want us to be so connected that I will know what He thinks before He speaks.

I give myself completely to God. Even if it means being cast out, cast down, beat up or beat down to the ground, I won't make a sound.
I am very much willing to be exhausted in this work for the souls to be saved.
Just to spread the gospel of the life that Christ gave.

Loving Him

I was put hear to evangelize the gospel of Jesus Christ. In doing this, I know I will pay the price.

However, the Word declares that Jesus overcame the world. Because I am an heir, I ain't scared.

God did not give us the spirit of fear but that of love, power, and a sound mind.
He has given me two thousand years ago the authority to bind Satan up.

All I have to do is walk in it, believe in it, and call upon the name above all names;
Jesus Christ, the Son of God, will He forever reign.

The Promise

With thanksgiving and gladness, my heart rejoices and sings in the Lord.
I soar higher and higher as my bones fill up with Holy Ghost fire. He cleanses me from head to toe so much I began to glow. To a new level of awesomeness, the Lord desires to take me - a freedom far beyond free, I'm I destined to be.

In the land His saints will begin to show up and show out....Oh yes, the ones who deeply believed and had no doubt. A generation He seeks that will worship Him in Spirit and Truth and not act cute. He is looking for a generation that will act in the authority given them and give Satan the boot.
He desires a generation that won't try to be of the world, and will count all things lost for Christ no matter the cost.
He longs for a generation that can go through just like Jesus had to...
One that won't talk out of both sides of their mouth, for the tongue is a powerful thing.
It will make you down south.
He is searching for a generation that want look down and frown for they know soon the trumpet is to sound.
Jesus Christ of Nazareth is looking for a generation that will praise Him, worship Him with all of their being, and not one that will have faith in what their seeing.
A crown of glory will be placed on this

generation's head.
His generation will be led to the wedding table and eternally fed.

The Experience

Have you ever been supersaturated by the anointing of the Holy Ghost? Your hands fly up and you can not speak, and only His face you overwhelmingly desire to seek. You want to run for the Son for what He has done. The Spirit man outruns the flesh. The flesh tries to hold you back but your spirit rises higher and higher with Holy Ghost fire. All you can do is exclaim, "Hallelujah, Praise God!!

Worship

Prophetic Worship

Twinkling lights all around,
Popping up here and there not making a sound.
As I worship and lift my hands in the air,
I see the hosts of heaven in a glare.
I strain my eyes to see angels worship God with me.
Dressed in gowns of flowing, crystal white,
Faces tinged with golden light.
They teach me Heavenly worship of which is out of courtship with the Father.

The cares of this world are not a bother, for I drift into the third Heaven.

Free from the earthly tent, I experience why Jesus was sent.
He came to save, not to condemn. He aches for us to be in His realm.
I worship in spirit and truth as I hear angels sing spiritual songs and hymns; crystal rays shoot across the room as the spirit of God pours like rain.
Jesus said, "For this reason did I endure
relentless pain.
Sorrows and death compassed Me about so much that I cried out.
I had to stay on there on the cross or the world would be lost.
My Father desired such to worship Him in
spirit and truth.

Loving Him

When you extended your hands in surrender with a heart to please, He chose you."

The Kiss

He kisses my finger tips and proceeds
towards my lips.
His glory envelops me as He looks into my eyes.

I sigh.

I part my lips and await His impartation.
He parts His lips and from them flow the Words of life.
As He imparts into me, the blackness of sin cascades from my heart.

Death is replaced with life.

He kisses my eyelids and my entire face as we embrace.
We do not haste in our loving. He raptures me into His secret place.

The New Jerusalem

I eat up the Lord. I drink the Lord, and I
soak Him up.
I put Him into me as much as I can.
Without His grace of fulfillment, I wouldn't be able
to stand.
I worship Him. I honor Him in the quietness of my
being so much I just exclaim, God!!!
I glory in Him, I wallow in His presence.
I am revived and recharged by His Holy Spirit as He
creeps in on me and takes me away.
I am supersaturated with His gloriousness and
majesty, and I am choked up by His awe.
I leave this world and partake of the newness
of His World.
Awesome, new, supersaturated, and Holy Ghost
filled Temple.
He Himself is the World.
I am lost in His World if only for a moment;
He is the World, and the World is God.

The Marriage

The flicker of His Eyes makes her heart skip a beat.
The train of His robe fills the temple as He takes
His place.
Crystal whiteness all around as the trumpets resound.
She is in awe at the flawlessness of His being for it is
that of clear ice with the radiance of the Son.
She looks and sees in the distance martyred saints
who feared none.
They come to the marriage ceremony casting their
golden crowns and arrayed in snow white apparel.
Crystal whiteness takes the place of their
wretched flesh.
A life of immorality will they live 'cause they passed
the test.
The Groomsman and His Father look at each other
with eyes of worship because these sons and daughters accepted Their Lordship.
At the wedding of bliss, Jesus bows and gives the
Church a kiss.

Heavenly Melodies

He is there before I extend my hands in worship.
He is there to kiss my fingertips.
As He kisses oh so gently my fingertips, glory shoots from them.
I am radiated by His Presence and engulfed
by His Essence.
I worship with my hands lifted up and a heart filled with praise; I am in a daze.
He teaches my hands to war.
My fingers are manipulated by the ripples that I see of His Presence.
The ripples turn into musical notes.
My fingers are the instruments.
I play and play and play…

The Worship of God

As I worship, He pours Himself on and in me. I see in the Spirit Him walking into my room. He comes and kneels down beside me to take a way the gloom. I feel Him moving in me as He touches my shoulder. I see angels all around dancing and prancing blowing trumpets of joy announcing the Lord's arrival. Tears fill my eyes and run down my face. Oh how I feel Him as I worship and praise His glorious and majestic name. As I worship Him, I'm loving Him.

I am in the third Heaven.

I feel worship all around; thunderous sounds fill the temple of the Lord. As we worship, smoke fills the temple from His glory. He is a wonder to behold and be with. I love Him as I worship; I worship Him! Oh, how I worship Him! Lightening and thunder proceed from His thrown. Rays of sunshine flood my way. It is Jesus welcoming me into His temple of God. Oh, how we worship and adore His name. His worthiness will I proclaim. I can see the Hand of God extend out of the cloud welcoming me. Along with the others around, we resound the praises of God. Oh, how I worship and adore His name. Him, I can feel. Him, I can taste. He surrounds me in a glory cloud. Oh, how I adore Him. Oh, how I long to be beside and in Him. Oh, how I worship and adore His name. He is worthy to be praised. I can hear the heartbeat of Him. I can

Loving Him

---

smell Him; He smells of purity beyond our human senses. So pristine is He that lives in me. He is clear as glass shining in the radiate sunshine. Oh, how I worship and love you God because you gave me love first while in your kingdom in the third Heaven.

Dance

As the shadow of the setting sun dances upon the ceiling so shall you dance before Me in heaven. You shall dance before Me day and night. You shall dance upon the table of My heart as an angel plays upon his harp.

In dancing, you are taught spiritual warfare. As you dance, the brilliance of My mind will be bestowed upon you.

Golden Rays

Golden rays fill the evening sky.
I see angels drawing nigh as I worship in the beauty of holiness.
The presence of God blankets me to protect me from Satan's lies.
I listen as trumpets sound.
The twenty-four elders casting golden crowns as all of heaven is in a high worship.

Golden rays fill the evening sky.
I see angels drawing nigh as I worship El Shaddai.
The presence of God moves in slowly as we honor the Lord of Glory.
I listen as the trumpets sound and watch as the heavenly rain comes down.
He washes all my cares away and pricks my heart so I can hear Him say its gonna be okay.

I'm Here

All of these words that I did speak remind you that My face you must continually seek.

As I pour My Spirit upon you as alabaster oil, I am sealing everything in you so you want be soiled by the ways of the world. Keeping you sealed and close to My heart is all I care to desire. I am He, the unquenchable fire.

Send praises up to Me like never before. Look to Me for everything as I cleanse you with My oil. I am with you this morning and will be tonight. In between the two, don't worry, you will be in My sight. I write this Psalm to you because I want you to remember what I have said. I want you to keep this knowledge of Me in your head. I want you to have a special place in My heart in which Satan knows for sure he can't tear us a part.

Even when you stop writing, I will continue to write on the table of your heart. My Spirit will be the pen, and I will whisper in your hearing through out the day. Now, I know your listening for My speech so that I can teach you who you are in Me and who you are to be. Look up My child even though the sun is not up. All you need is the Son to pour into your cup. Overflowing happiness He will bring. Sweet songs of Zion will He sing.

Divine Perseverance

As I stand in the glow of His light, His hand caresses my face.
He lovingly says my child it's going to be alright despite the trials and tribulations coming your way.
By shedding My blood on the cross, did I pay for it to be okay.
I understand the sadness and frustration of the heart.
You wish that hard times would just part. Remember what I had to go through?
I was pierced in the hands and feet after they
beat Me.
You see I took all of that for you.
Honey, my love for you is true.
I understood that my blood would cover a multitude of pain in you.
In this, I am not ashamed.
Please lay hold of my claim that you are my heir.
I know that this position want take a way your cares but trust Me, honey, your heartaches will I
always bare.

Momma Died

Uncaring filled my heart when my momma died; a lonely world I felt I would forever reside, but a sparkle of hope filled my desolate soul. The Holy Spirit began to flow. In His flowing, He captured all of my sadness and turned it into gladness.

Jesus came and sat with me on the floor. His position denotes that He still has authority over death, hell and the grave. He put His loving Arms around me as I cried. In Him and the Father did I abide. While enveloped in His glory did my weeping cease. I sensed Him saying peace child peace. Your mother is not in any pain or sorrow. You have to learn how to live for tomorrow for I am the Resurrection and the Truth and the Life. Continue abiding in Me and you'll be alright. It is done. Your mission is complete. You preached My gospel to your mother. You ministered to her and you loved her. It seemed at times that salvation would never occur. You witnessed the gospel to her. You submitted yourself to Me because in Me do you fear. When submission seemed so tough, you cried and I gave you My love. Only the anointing from above has kept you and will continue. Your efforts have not been in vain despite what Satan has been saying.

Loving Him

Unhindered Love

As I stand in the pool of His glory, listen as I tell you the story of our love affair….

A light had shone from heaven above all around me. He said, "Daughter come in to me for I want to penetrate the very fiber of your being. You need the impartation from me to cure your sin. You have been with only mere men. Come into Me. A love I've got for you that will cause you to be free. I see that you desire a physical love. Since I am from above, this I am unable to give. A thrill in the Spirit is what you need to kill that flesh. Your legs I do not wish for you to open, but a heart that is hoping that I will take you to a place of escape. I know you have been raped. Be not nervous from the Ultimate Lover's Hands, for I can touch you in places you did not know you had. I will replace bad images with pure love from above. I do not wish to rub your physical body in perfumed oils or kiss it 'til your toes coil. I give you the Holy Spirit who is the anointing. He is the Ultimate oil from Heaven. Instead of sweet smelling perfumes, He will become a stench in the nostrils of demons. Instead of a kiss, He will be the energy that will keep you going through out a life time. I do not wish to climb your body but this is My promise to you. I promise that you shall mount up with wings as an eagle, soaring…. I want to give My love to you. Our love will not be earthly. It can not be because we are spiritual beings. I

Loving Him

will take you to places that mere humans can not even imagine. Come in to me, you'll see."

Worship

I love Him so. He comes when I whisper His name. He drenches me in His rain. Every part of me worships Him in spirit and in truth. His glory touches my eyes, and I see angels gone up in a high worship. His glory kisses my lips, and I am endowed with Heaven's power. My tent does not prevent my escape into His presence. Burdens are lifted as I am hurled into the third heaven.

Healing Virtue

Jesus comes into my room as I lye on my bed in sickly gloom. I see in the Spirit Hands coming towards me. He gently places His massive Hands upon my head, and rubs my hair. He begins to bear the sickness of my body. Drenched in His healing virtue, the weakness starts to dissipate. I am no longer weak but strong. Even more of Him inhabits me. I can see in the midst of His glory. I can see visions of where He and I are to go in this life. It does not matter if no one else goes, for I am betrothed to His Spirit as His wife. I long for Him to constantly overflow me. Being in His presence is no mystery for I can feel the movement of His presence quickening my once weak flesh. My body quakes and shakes as He floods me. My spirit moans and groans. I whisper I love you. Death hath lost her sting. I am comforted by Him as He takes my breath a way. My eyes roll back as my body shakes and quakes as the Holy Spirit envelopes me.

The Triumph of Jesus

All I have to do is whisper to Him. He immediately comes to see about me. His presence floods me so that I see angels worshiping in Heaven. Sounds of trumpets are heard in the distance. He enters my heart and fills my soul. The majesty of God fills the land. Everything is filled with music...

Oh no what is happening? A thunderous sound is heard in the land. A band of angels on horseback come into sight. They are geared and ready to fight. Satan squeals with fright. The angels stomp on the ground and lightening shoots out from their feet. Satan gets his demons and they prepare to leave. Who do I see in the mist of the battle? It is Jesus on his horse and saddle. He speaks and the atmosphere becomes a blaze. As the saints shout, Satan is put in a daze. The hosts of heaven worship, and the saints praise as Satan is paid for the hurt that he gave. Roped, tied up and thrown into the lake of fire, Satan quickly expires. The saints shout with praise as Jesus summons them to take their rightful place. In His presence, they will forever abide. In their mansions in glory, will they forever reside.